Teaching

The Heart of God's Redemptive Program

James M. "Buck" Hatch

Columbia International University
Columbia, South Carolina

Teaching: The Heart of God's Redemptive Program

7435 Monticello Rd.
Columbia, SC 29203
www.ciu.edu

Columbia International University exists to train men and women from a biblical world view to impact the nations with the message of Christ through service in the marketplace, missions and the local church.

This book is based on a lecture series first transcribed and published by BCM International, Inc. (formerly Bible Club Movement, Inc.)
www.bcmintl.org

Editing, cover and interior layout by Kelly Smith, Tallgrass Media. Cover photo © Frannyanne, www.dreamstime.com

ISBN-13: 978-1-939074-01-0

Contents

Foreword

In the mid-1980s, the Bible Club Movement (known to-day as BCM International) invited Columbia International University professor James "Buck" Hatch to address its annual conference on the topic of teaching and learning. CIU was later granted permission to transcribe his teaching sessions for use within its Bible teaching programs. This material is now being reintroduced in the form of this book, as a "classic" resource.

Mr. Hatch's insights and framework are as powerful today as when first presented, and the pages of this book provide a philosophical foundation for a new generation of Christian educators. The ideas are enduring because they are biblical, and thus not only true, but timeless.

This work appeared prior to an emphasis by the educational community on learning styles, differentiated learning, brain-based learning and culturally responsive teaching, and yet each of these "researched-based" instructional paradigms are grounded in the truths presented within Mr. Hatch's model. The importance of a knowledge of the learner, student involvement and engagement, under-standing, and motivation as outlined by Mr. Hatch have endured and are an integral to contemporary educational ideas and strategies.

During the formative years of my career I was given a copy of this philosophy of teaching and learning as a resource for developing a Christian instructional philosophy. Having completed a graduate degree in education at a secular university, I understood the latest trends and models for curriculum and instruction, but I was grappling with whether or not these ideas aligned with biblical truth. Mr. Hatch's "training model" provided a needed frame of reference. I continue to use the concepts from this paradigm to assist the next generation of Christian educators in developing their philosophy of teaching and learning.

Christian schools strive to be excellent academically, but also spiritually through programs grounded in the Word of God, curriculum and instructional practices where Christ is the coherence factor, and a faculty that understands the importance of incarnational teaching. Christian educators, across the spectrum of Christian education, have a renewed interest in making their classrooms "transformational" through the process of spiritual formation. This book is a classic in that it continues to speak clearly to the desired outcomes of our contemporary classrooms. For this reason it will become a resource within the Lowrie Center for Christian School Education at CIU and assist the center in its mission to perpetuate the enduring ideas upon which Christian schooling was founded.

In his conclusion Mr. Hatch refers to the teaching process as complex, and rightly so, but he was known for his humble and yet dynamic ability to bring clarity to complexity. He provided understanding by living out the principles of this book in the context of the classroom and through relationships with his students. Countless students have been "moved" and "changed" through an understanding of this model of biblical teaching and learning. It is my sincere prayer that this legacy will continue as the principles are shared with a new generation of Christian educators.

Dr. Milton V. Uecker
Director, Lowrie Center for Christian School Education
College of Education
Columbia International University
www.lowriecenter.com

Chapter 1

Teaching or Training?

A Definition of Teaching

One of the most helpful things in understanding how to teach is to clarify what teaching is. Because of our past experiences, many of us have faulty ideas connected with the word "teach." It is so often tied with the idea of talking and listening. The teacher talks and the student listens. This, we say, is "teaching." So, if the students listen quietly and information is transmitted in such a way that it can be recited, we conclude that adequate teaching is going on. Yet the Word of God presents something entirely different and calls it teaching. There is another word in our vernacular that comes closer to the biblical concept, and that is the word "training."

What does "training" suggest to you? Does it not have a different connotation than "teaching"? During military training, for instance, one can be sure that there is more going on than just talking. That is part of the process, but the the chief training component is out on the field.

Let me illustrate the meaning of training with this simple picture of a railroad train.

The word "train", referring to the locomotive, comes from the same root as the word we are using as a substitute for teaching. To see this, note what the engine does. It does not just sit and talk to the cars. If it is going to Philadelphia, it is not fulfilling its function as a train unless it pulls the cars from where they are to Philadelphia. This engine is the teacher and the cars are the students. "Training", in its root meaning, is "to pull along." A train is a series of cars pulled along by an engine.

Training is thus the process in which one person takes another person, in his behavior, to the place where the first person already is. The behavior of one person, the student, is changed into conformity with a standard exemplified by another, the teacher.

This is the essence of the redemptive concern of God. He said, "and be holy, for I am holy" (Lev. 11:44). Through His training, "we all, with unveiled face, beholding the glory of the Lord, are being transformed into the same image from one degree of glory to another" (2 Cor. 3:18). As an instrument in His hand, I should not be satisfied that I am teaching unless there is a change in my students in terms of the standard.

Chapter 2

The Standard for the Teaching Process

As found in Christ

If we accept this definition of teaching, then more is involved than just talking and listening. If teaching is the process of bringing the behavior of a child into conformity to the standards of the Word, then more time is needed than the usual twenty minutes of Sunday school. If a teacher is to change another's life, then more demands are put upon him or her than the skills of transmitting information.

In this approach to the teaching process there will be a strong emphasis on the student. In our train analogy, there has to be a change in the "cars." To travel from Pottstown to Philadelphia, they must do more than merely "sit and listen." They must move. They must change. This is what is before us: how to produce these changes.

It is not surprising that authorities are not agreed as to the best method of carrying on this complex process of changing the behavior of another. In many cases the problem lies in the fact that the teachers do not know where they want to take their students. Among the many voices of educational philosophy, there is a desperate need for an authoritative voice saying, "This is the way, walk in it" (Isa. 30:21). One would think that God would have given us such, since teaching is such a vital part of his work. And he has done this in the person of his Son. The Lord

Jesus is our authoritative example not only in life but also in service. One who would know how to teach needs only to walk in his steps, for he is the Master Teacher. Let us consider him as our standard not only how to live but also how to teach.

There is a widespread attitude among Christians that if you want to understand spiritual or moral things you go to the Word of God and the Lord Jesus. On the other hand, if you want to know how to teach or to understand human behavior, you go to a human authority in the field. May I suggest a better way? In recent decades great insights have been gained in the fields of human behavior. These are not to be ignored. Yet Christian teachers should not expect these to do more than they are designed to do. These are natural principles and are effective in producing natural results. In Christian teaching, supernatural changes are necessary, so the Christian teacher needs more than these natural principles. In the Lord Jesus one finds the supernatural principles of teaching along with the natural in a balance that only God could give. As we observe him in his methods, we will see every valid teaching principle ever discovered by men and much more.

Our basic approach then, is to follow the Lord Jesus as our authority in teaching methods. "But," someone may say, "It has just been in my lifetime that people have been using flannel board and object lessons. Why, surely these are modern discoveries." Yet when we consider more deeply, we are overwhelmed with the wonder of the fact that the first object lessons were planned by God Himself ages ago. The Tabernacle in the Old Testament was an elaborate object lesson, and all of creation is a great flannel board pointing by analogy to the great truths of redemption. The Lord Jesus pointed to this in his parables and made constant use of illustration in his teaching. If you would know how to teach, study the Bible and follow the Lord Jesus, not only in his message but also in his method.

Chapter 3

Rules for the Teaching Process: The Teacher

As we have seen, teaching may be understood as a process by which one person brings the behavior of another person to where it is supposed to be. One is not teaching unless there is an appropriate change in the behavior of the students. The Lord Jesus did this when he taught his disciples to pray, modeling a pattern to follow. Our authoritative standard for training others in the ways of God is the Lord Jesus himself. We turn now to the first rule about teaching, which may be observed clearly in Christ.

All through the Bible God puts forth a principle of teaching that man tends to overlook. In God's ways it is much more important what the teacher *is* than what the teacher *does*. In man's ways, flowing from a heart that considers itself right and "treat[s] others with contempt" (Luke 18:9), the tendency is to think the main need is in the student. God reverses this and indicates that if the teacher is what they ought to be, many of the problems of teaching are solved. Our "train" clearly illustrates this. If the cars are not moving in the right direction, one looks first to see if the engine is moving in that direction. The Lord Jesus may have had this in mind when he said, "Take my yoke upon you, and learn from me, for I am gentle and lowly in heart" (Matt. 11:29). The Bible puts great importance on this matter and warns, "Not many of you should become teachers, my brothers, for you know that we who teach will be judged with greater strictness" (James 3:1). We cannot cover all that the Bible says of the teacher, but we shall consider several basic points illustrated in the life of the Lord Jesus.

Quality 1: Trust in God

The first responsibility of the teacher is seen in the Lord Jesus as he describes himself in John 8:28, "When you have lifted up the Son of Man, then you will know that I am he, and that I do nothing on my own authority." Twice before in the Gospel of John he says, that "the Son can do nothing of his own accord" (John 5:19, 30). The Lord is presented here as the Son of God, and yet he says that he can do nothing himself. The rest of John 8:28 gives further light on the meaning of this as Jesus says that he speaks "as the Father taught me." Did Jesus have the ability to do anything? He certainly did, for he was God. Then what did he mean that he could "do nothing on [his] own authority"? I think he meant this. It was as if he were saying, "In order to show my disciples in all ages how to do everything, including teaching, I am going show them the way they must do it. Though I have the ability as God I will not touch that. Not trusting my own ability I will trust the Father to work through me."

Here is the first requirement of a teacher who would be like the Lord Jesus. Regardless of any natural ability or knowledge, he or she must trust in the Lord with all their heart. Behind this is the fact that none of us is sufficient to change the life of another in the area of the things of God. Only God can do that. It is only reasonable that we must trust God to do what only God can do.

Quality 2: Commitment to Prayer

The second quality of a good teacher is closely related

to the first one. This will probably not mean much to one for whom the first quality is not real. In the last verse of John 7 and the first verse of John 8 we read, "they went each to his own house, but Jesus went to the Mount of Olives." Do you know why he went to the mountain? The next verse says, "early in the morning he came again to the temple. All the people came to him, and he sat down and taught them" (John 8:2). Do you know what he did on the mountain? He was preparing for his teaching the next morning. How? Do you think he had his books before him in study? This type of preparation is necessary but not as basic what he was doing. It seems clear from similar passages that he was praying all night. Jesus prayed because he knew the Father must do the work.

We will never pray as Jesus prayed until we are absolutely convinced that we can do nothing of ourselves. This came as a shock to me one day. I often wondered why I prayed so little. Then someone said in passing, "The reason we don't pray is because we are trusting ourselves." If I can do it, then there is no point in praying. If I cannot do it and I know no one who can, then it is despair. Yet if I know I cannot do it but have a God who is able and has promised to do it, then I will pray.

Let me ask you who have been teaching, "How much time do you usually spend in preparation for a teaching opportunity?" The shocking question comes when I ask myself how much of this time is spent in study and how much in prayer. I am sure we would all see more real results if we spent as much time praying as we did studying. This is the second thing we see in our model teacher: he prayed. The teacher must be dependent upon the Lord instead of abilities, knowledge or methods. And he or she must be a person of prayer.

Quality 3: Teaching from God's Authority

In Matthew 5 we see another occasion on which the Lord Jesus was teaching and he demonstrated a third characteristic of a good teacher. "Seeing the crowds, he went up on the mountain, and when he sat down, his disciples came to him. And he opened his mouth and taught them . . ." (v. 1-2). The Lord Jesus did talk but that is not all he did. In Matthew 7:28 we read, "when Jesus finished these sayings, the crowds were astonished at his teaching." They had never had a teacher like this. The thing that struck them was that "he was teaching them as one who had authority, and not as their scribes" (v. 29).

Here was a man that was absolutely convinced in his own soul that what he was giving was the truth. He was not giving out something he had heard someone else say, but that which he knew from his own experience to be truth. When the scribes taught, they would quote this one and that one, but they had no convictions of their own. In this day of many books about the Bible we are in danger of being like the scribes. We need the help of other people of God, but their understandings of the truth of God cannot be a substitute for our own convictions borne by the Holy Spirit out of the Word of God. When God has deeply convinced us that this is the truth, and burned it into our souls, then we can stand up with authority and speak with deep conviction. It will be like the blind man who proclaimed, "one thing I do know, that though I was blind, now I see" (John 9:25). Thus the teacher who is like the Lord will be prayerful and depending on God. As he does this, the Holy Spirit causes him to know the things of God. Then, and only then, can he speak with authority.

Quality 4: Teaching by Example

The next characteristic of a good teacher we see demonstrated by the Lord Jesus in John 13. On this occasion he taught his disciples a very important lesson. Note carefully how he did it. The opening words of this chapter tell us something very wonderful about him. "Jesus, knowing that the Father had given all things into his hands, and that he had come from God and was going back to God . . ." (v. 3). If this were true of you, how would you teach? And how would you teach this particular lesson? Now watch how he did it. "He laid aside his outer garments, and taking a towel, tied it around his waist" (v. 4). This was not a "towel" in our sense of the word but more like an apron of a household slave. "When he had washed their feet and put on his outer garments and resumed his place, he said to them, 'Do you understand what I have done to you?'" (v. 12)

Do you see the lesson for that hour? He was teaching his disciples godly humility and he demonstrated a basic principle of teaching in an amazing way. He who was the Son of God and "heir of all things" taught humility by humbling himself to wash his disciples' feet. If we would teach as Jesus taught, we must show in our lives an incarnation of the truth that are trying to teach our students. God's way of teaching is to "show and tell."

Chapter 4

Rules for the Teaching Process: The Student

The life of the teacher is basic in the teaching process. In dealing with the things of God, one cannot teach if he is not being taught. Even as the Master Teacher said prophetically of himself, "The Lord God has given me the tongue of those who are taught, that I may know how to sustain with a word him who is weary. Morning by morning he awakens; he awakens my ear to hear as those who are taught" (Is. 50:4). And yet teaching is not just being something; it is taking another person to the place where they should be. In our illustration, it is not enough for the engine to go to Philadelphia; it must take the cars with it or there is no train. This brings us to the next vital aspect of the teaching process. As the engine must be "coupled" with the cars, so the teacher must be so involved with the students that they will follow.

The Need to Become Involved

This teacher-student relationship is sometimes called "understanding the learner" but that underscores only the mental aspect. It may be called "acceptance of the learner," but this is merely the volitional component. It is often thought of as "loving the student", but this is the emotional aspect. The reality seems to be the total involvement of one person (teacher) with another total person (student). It is even as "the soul of Jonathan was knit to the soul of

David" (1 Sam. 18:1). In good teaching, there must be some degree of this mutual involvement.

How did the Lord Jesus interact with children? In Mark 10:13 we read, "they were bringing children to him . . . and the disciples rebuked them." Do you think the disciples were interested in these children? Oh, no! But watch the Lord Jesus. "But when Jesus saw it, he was indignant and said to them, 'Let the children come to me; do not hinder them, for to such belongs the kingdom of God. Truly, I say to you, whoever does not receive the kingdom of God like a child shall not enter it.' And he took them in his arms and blessed them, laying his hands on them" (Mark 10:14-16). Did the Lord Jesus love, accept, understand children? Oh, what understanding he had! If you are to teach, you have to be involved with people or you will never connect with them and take them to your goal.

Now let's look at a passage where we find an example of a group of teachers who did not understand the person, and also an occasion where the Lord Jesus demonstrated the fact that he did understand. Out of this situation, we will see that the Lord Jesus not only understands, but he wants us to understand our students.

In John 8, the Lord Jesus, knowing that he was going to teach the next day, went to the Mount of Olives, apparently to pray all night. Prepared to teach, he came down early the next morning. Now observe those who came to hear him. They are the would-be teachers!

"Early in the morning he came again to the temple. All the people came to him, and he sat down and taught them. The scribes and the Pharisees brought a woman who had been caught in adultery . . ." (John 8:2-3). Who were the scribes and Pharisees? They were the ones who should have been teaching the people! One of the lessons they should have been teaching was, "Thou shalt not commit adultery." Now watch the way they taught, and may the Lord deliver us from this kind of teaching.

"The scribes and the Pharisees brought a woman who had been caught in adultery, and placing her in the midst . . ." (John 8:3). Do you think that the scribes and Pharisees cared personally about her? Have you ever, by a look of the face or a tone of the voice, picked out a poor little child because he hasn't learned, and done what they did to this poor woman, seeking to make them an example? Have you ever seen a teacher do that?

They took the woman caught in the act of adultery and stood her up there in the midst of these religious people. How would you feel? Do you think you would be in a position to learn anything? A person will never learn anything that way. Oh, what teachers!

They said to him, "Teacher, this woman has been caught in the act of adultery. Now in the Law Moses commanded us to stone such women. So what do you say?" (v. 4-5). Did they have an objective moral standard, a goal to which they were supposed to take their students? Sure they did, but they were not concerned about teaching this woman anything. "This they said to test him, that they might have some charge to bring against him" (v. 6). Jesus stooped down and wrote something on the ground with his finger.

Now let's skip to the end of the story and see how the Lord Jesus dealt with this woman. "Jesus stood up and said to her, 'Woman, where are they? Has no one condemned you?'" (v. 10). Oh, may the Lord give us this understanding of people! Can you hear the voice, can you feel the heart, can you see the look on his face as he turned to her? She saw it, she felt it. She forgot where she was, she forgot everything except this wonderful teacher who understood her and all of her need and all of her problems. "She said, 'No one, Lord.' And Jesus said, 'Neither do I condemn you; go, and from now on sin no more'" (v. 11). Do you think she ever committed adultery again? Never!

Earlier when the teachers were testing him, did he lift up himself, and say them, "What you need is to understand this woman!" No, he did not say that. Watch what he says, "Let him who is without sin among you be the first to throw a stone at her" (v. 7). Now do you know what he was telling them? Simply this – they didn't understand people, and the reason is because there was sin in their hearts. He pointed to their sin, and they all, without exception, turned away and walked out.

Do you want to understand people? I will tell you God's method. The chief part of understanding people is given to you in these simple verses I want to leave with you. When the Lord began to show me this, I was teaching a class on educational psychology. I asked the students, "Do you know of any occasion where a teacher did not understand you as a person and, because they did not understand you, did something that hindered your learning?" They told story after story, and I could add many more examples from my own experience. I remember when I was studying Latin, and the Latin teacher stood up one day, snapped her finger and said, "Square yourself, young man, and stand up there and conjugate that verb!" I wilted and I cried, and in sheer humiliation I left the room. I know I was at fault, but she didn't understand me.

Then I asked the students another question. Would a person who was filled with and under the control of the Holy